Legends of Rock

The BEATLES
Defining Rock 'n' Roll

by Joe Tougas

Consultant: Meredith Rutledge-Borger
Associate Curator
Rock and Roll Hall of Fame & Museum
Cleveland, Ohio

CAPSTONE PRESS
a capstone imprint

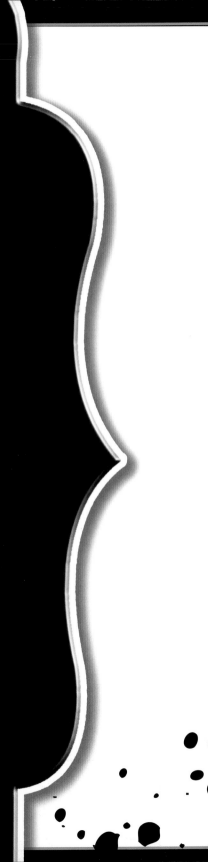

Edge Books are published by Capstone Press,
1710 Roe Crest Drive, North Mankato, Minnesota 56003
www.capstonepub.com

Library of Congress Cataloging-in-Publication Data
Tougas, Joe.
   The Beatles: defining rock 'n' roll / by Joe Tougas.
       pages cm. — (Edge. Legends of rock.)
   Includes bibliographical references and index.
   Summary: "Describes the rise to fame and the lasting impact of
the band The Beatles"— Provided by publisher.
   ISBN 978-1-4914-1816-1 (library binding)
   ISBN 978-1-4914-1821-5 (ebook pdf)
   1. Beatles—Juvenile literature. 2. Rock musicians—England—
Biography—Juvenile literature. I. Title.
   ML3930.B35T68 2015
   782.421660922'2-dc23 [B]   2014023794

Editorial Credits
Mandy Robbins, editor; Tracy Davies-McCabe, designer; Eric Gohl,
media researcher; Gene Bentdahl, production specialist

Primary Source Quotes
p. 4, Rolling Stone magazine, July 24, 2012; p. 7 interview on
Tom Snyder's television show, Tomorrow, NBC, April 1975; p. 16, 19,
24, The Beatles' Anthology

Photo Credits
Alamy: Pictorial Press Ltd, 21, 22-23, 25; AP Photo: 5, Dan
Grossi, cover; Getty Images: Michael Ochs Archives, 16 (bottom),
Popperfoto, 17; Glow Images: Everett Collection, 18, Land of Lost
Content, 24; Newscom: KRT/Handout, 4, Mirrorpix, 19, Mirrorpix/
Daily Mirror, 13, Reuters/Mario Anzuoni, 28-29, WENN Photos/PFI,
26-27, ZUMA Press, 20, ZUMA Press/KEYSTONE Pictures USA,
8-9, 10-11, 14-15; Shutterstock: catwalker, 6 (middle), Ivan Cholakov,
6 (top), meaofoto, 7, Spirit of America, 6 (bottom), Victor Torres, 26
(inset)

Design Elements
Shutterstock

Printed in the United States of America in
Stevens Point, Wisconsin.
092014   008479WZS15

Table of Contents

"So Let Me Introduce to You..."

"From one generation to the next, The Beatles will remain the most important rock band of all time."

-Dave Grohl, lead singer of the Foo Fighters

Many music lovers would agree that in rock 'n' roll music, there are the Beatles, and everything else. Elvis Presley, Buddy Holly, and others got rock rolling in the late 1950s. They made strong impressions on four Liverpool, England, teenagers: John Lennon, Paul McCartney, George Harrison, and Ringo Starr.

The four young men would become the Beatles. The group first grew famous in England for their upbeat live performances. Fans swooned, shrieked, and even fainted. When the band arrived in the United States in 1964 to perform on TV, 73 million viewers tuned in. Americans were treated to shockingly good new music and four men who were creative, thoughtful, and surprisingly funny.

With perfect vocal work, clever lyrics, and unusual song structures, the Beatles influenced countless musicians. Their creativity also inspired a *generation* of young people to find new ways to express themselves.

In their 10 years together, the Beatles always challenged themselves. They took chances instead of following trends. By doing this they made music that continues to entertain, amaze, and inspire people around the world.

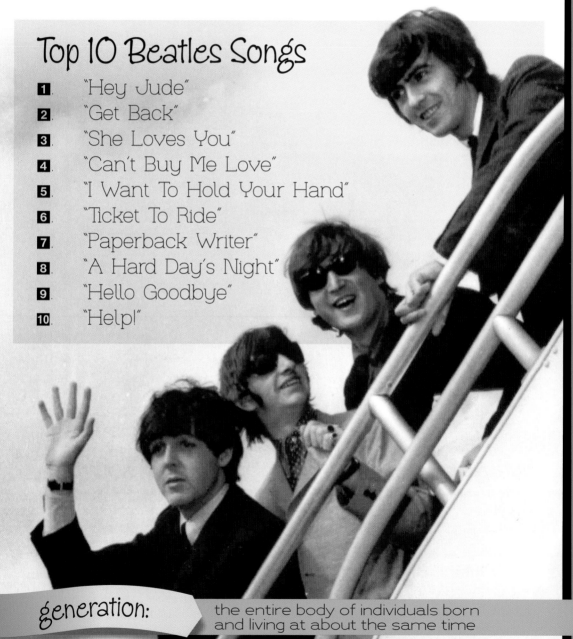

Top 10 Beatles Songs

1. "Hey Jude"
2. "Get Back"
3. "She Loves You"
4. "Can't Buy Me Love"
5. "I Want To Hold Your Hand"
6. "Ticket To Ride"
7. "Paperback Writer"
8. "A Hard Day's Night"
9. "Hello Goodbye"
10. "Help!"

generation: the entire body of individuals born and living at about the same time

The Early BEATLES

1

The four boys who became the Beatles were born at a time when their city was being torn apart by bombs. Liverpool, England, was often a target of German air raids during World War II (1939–1945). Paul McCartney's parents actually met during an air strike as they took shelter in a basement.

Watching and Learning

The Beatles did not meet one another until the late 1950s. By then they had each become fascinated by early American rock 'n' roll music. Songs by Buddy Holly, Little Richard, and especially Elvis Presley excited them. Elvis sang songs that sounded like the African-American rhythm and blues he admired growing up in Memphis, Tennessee. He sang with a range from low mumbling to high-pitched squeals. It often looked like the music was taking over his entire body. He would shake, twist, and shout in concerts and movies. The future Beatles paid close attention.

"They'd all scream when he came on the screen," John Lennon said of seeing Elvis movies as a teenager. "So we thought 'That's a good job!'"

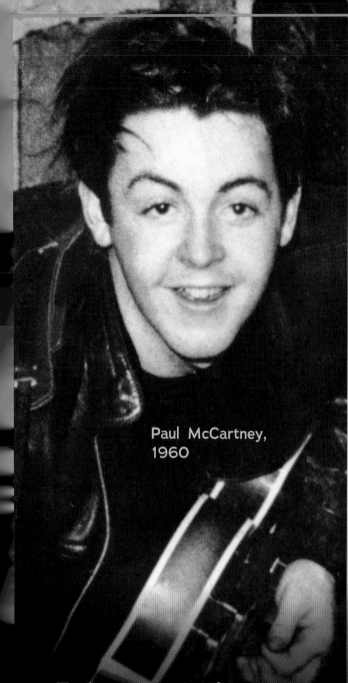

Paul McCartney, 1960

Backstage Pass

Paul McCartney

Born: June 18, 1942, in Liverpool, England

Role: vocals, bass guitar, guitar, piano, drums

What he brought to the group: Paul is famous for singing and songwriting. But he also played bass guitar with a busy but clean style that gave a colorful sound to Beatles songs.

Backstage Pass

John Lennon

Born: Oct. 9, 1940, in Liverpool, England

Died: Dec. 8, 1980, in New York City

Role: vocals, rhythm guitar, bass guitar

What he brought to the group: John was a creative rebel. As a guitar player and songwriter, he was always searching for something new and meaningful.

John Meets Paul

John Lennon was raised by his aunt, Mimi Smith. At first she did not approve of him spending so much time playing music. But she was moved by his love for music and later claimed to have bought John his first guitar. John would later recall it being bought by his mother, Julia.

John Lennon,
1960

harmony: a set of musical notes played or sung at the same time; the notes blend together to form harmony

In 1957 John formed a band called the Quarry Men. This group of friends began learning and playing the American rock 'n' roll songs they heard on late-night radio.

At a Quarry Men performance at a church festival, John was introduced to another guitar player, Paul McCartney. Paul knew plenty about rock 'n' roll. He also enjoyed the music of the Everly Brothers, who sang with amazing vocal **harmony.**

Paul joined the band and became good friends with John. Soon the two were writing their own songs while learning and rehearsing others. Paul introduced the Quarry Men to a younger friend of his, George Harrison. At first, John protested having somebody three years younger in his band. But George's lead guitar playing spoke for itself. He soon became a member.

The Quarry Men had several people join and leave the band. They changed their name several times before deciding on the Beatles. The group became a local favorite. They blended the wild spirit of American rock 'n' roll with vocal harmonies that were perfectly on pitch. Soon the entire country would be paying attention.

The early Beatles from left to right:
George Harrison, Pete Best (original drummer),
Paul McCartney, John Lennon

Backstage Pass

George Harrison

Born: Feb. 25, 1943,
in Liverpool, England
Died: Nov. 29, 2001,
in Beverly Hills, California
Role: lead guitar, vocals, sitar
What he brought to the group:
From the start George's guitar
playing added texture that
drew from many different
styles. He later developed into
a gifted songwriter.

2 From BBC to OVERSEAS

As their fame spread past Liverpool in 1961 and 1962, the Beatles hired a manager named Brian Epstein. Brian helped the band get a large British record company, Electrical and Musical Industries (EMI), to record them. By this time the Beatles had replaced their drummer, Pete Best, with Ringo Starr.

The band's second single, "Please Please Me," went to Number One on the British Broadcasting Corporation (BBC) pop charts in early 1963. This cheerful song showed off John, Paul, and George's three-part harmonies over a quirky but catchy rhythm. Their record producer, George Martin, loved how naturally the Beatles sang and wrote songs.

Backstage Pass

Brian Epstein

Born: Sept 19, 1934,
    in Liverpool, England
Died: August 27, 1967
Role: manager
What he brought to the group:
Considered the "fifth Beatle,"
Epstein was the one who first
believed in the young band.
He worked behind the scenes to
get record companies interested.

Backstage Pass

George Martin

Born: Jan 3, 1926, in London
Role: record producer/engineer
What he brought to the group:
Martin was as creative in the
control room as the Beatles
were in the recording studio.
His many ideas improved the
Beatles' recordings. These ideas
included using sounds seldom
heard in rock 'n' roll, such as
harpsichords and full orchestras.

The Beatles and manager Brian Epstein arrive home from Paris in 1964.

Backstage Pass

Ringo Starr

Real Name: Richard Starkey
Born: July 7, 1940,
            in Liverpool, England
Role: drums, vocals
What he brought to the group:
Ringo had a great knack for
filling a song's space with
exciting blasts of drum passages.
He gave depth and power to
songs such as "She Loves You"
and "Please Please Me."

harpsichord: a keyboard instrument similar to a piano; a harpsichord has wire strings that are plucked rather than being struck like the strings in a piano

Beatlemania

The Beatles' first album for EMI showed they had plenty more to offer fans. Fans screamed with delight at live performances in Liverpool, London, and other cities in Great Britain. The crowd noise eventually caused problems for the Beatles, but early on they loved the attention. British newspapers and magazines began calling this craze "Beatlemania."

Paul McCartney, John Lennon, and George Harrison blend vocals to create the Beatles' unmistakeable harmonies.

In 1964 Beatlemania overran the United States. While eager to perform in the land of their musical heroes, the Beatles waited until they had a Number One song there. It happened in February 1964 when the Lennon-McCartney song "I Want To Hold Your Hand" topped the U.S. charts. That same month, the Beatles were set to appear on the CBS Sunday

The British Invasion

The Beatles' plane landed at New York City's JFK airport on February 7, 1964. The four "lads from Liverpool" stepped off the plane to the sight and sound of thousands of cheering fans welcoming them. Two days later 73 million viewers tuned in for their performance on *The Ed Sullivan Show*. The appearance set a world record for TV audiences.

"we thought we'd have to work a little harder than this."

-George Harrison referring to Beatlemania in the United States

The Beatles greet fans upon arriving in New York City.

"Let Me See You Smile"

The Beatles' TV appearance let Americans see the musicians whose songs were suddenly heard all over the radio. And what a sight! The Beatles were enthusiastic when they played. They shook their shaggy hair while hitting high notes, triggering screams from their fans. They were clearly having as much fun as the young people watching them.

Many adults saw the Beatles as long-haired screamers who made noise instead of music. But to millions of young Americans, the Beatles delivered a fresh sound and an upbeat attitude. Only months before, President John F. Kennedy was shot and killed. This event spread gloom over the entire nation. Many young people felt sadness and confusion over his loss. In the United States the Beatles found an audience eager for a reason to smile again.

Making Recording HISTORY

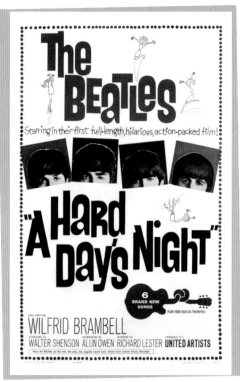

By the mid-1960s the Beatles were bigger than their own musical heroes. They sold millions of records. In April of 1964, the band had the top five singles in America. By August 1965 they had starred in two movies and released seven albums in the United States. Six became Number One hits.

After the Shouting, a Twist

With their popularity, though, came problems. Beatlemania made playing at concerts difficult. From 1964 to 1966 the band performed around the world. They were eager to play new songs such as "Baby's In Black" and "Nowhere Man." But too often the only sound to be heard came from the roar of the fans. The fans were often louder than the band. What was once fun for the Beatles became a struggle. Audience members could barely hear the band, and the Beatles themselves could not hear one another play. The band feared they were turning in terrible performances as a result.

"It's like a riot, not a show..."

-John Lennon, referring to a Beatles concert

Fans went crazy for the Beatles. Some screamed, cried, and lost all control.

After a 1966 show in San Francisco, the Beatles decided to stop giving concerts and to put their energy into the recording studio. Along with their very creative producer, George Martin, the Beatles began making some of the most unique and memorable records in music history.

Opening Doors and Minds

By the late 1960s, John and Paul were writing songs about more than just love and girls. They were exploring darker feelings such as loneliness, fear, and feeling out of place. These themes made for much stronger, more unique songs. George Harrison was writing as well, sometimes using a sitar, a stringed instrument from India. The Beatles were now gaining an even larger audience. New fans liked the band's imagination. Fans also enjoyed how the Beatles experimented with different styles, including touches of **psychedelic** music.

A high point of this phase came in 1967 with Paul's idea to record an album pretending to be a different group. The result was *Sgt. Pepper's Lonely Hearts Club Band*, a record with an odd combination of sounds. Some songs used circus music while others used a full orchestra. Some lyrics were simple and sweet:

George Harrison playing a sitar

"Do you believe in a love at first sight? Yes, I'm certain that it happens all the time."

Some were more like reading dream-like poetry:

"cellophane flowers of yellow and green, towering over your head ..."

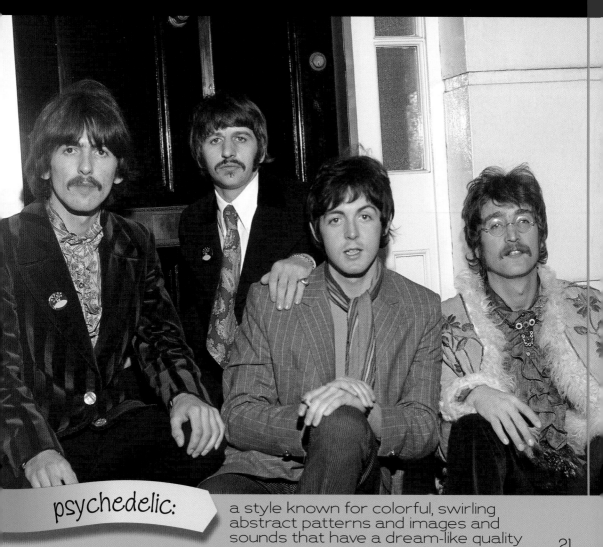

psychedelic: a style known for colorful, swirling abstract patterns and images and sounds that have a dream-like quality

Serious Talent

Sgt. Pepper is the Beatles' masterpiece. In 2012 *Rolling Stone* magazine ranked it as the best album of all time. The magazine called it "the most important rock 'n' roll album ever made." Three other Beatles albums made the magazine's top 10 albums of all time. *Revolver* came in third, *Rubber Soul* fifth, and *The Beatles* (also known as *The White Album*) 10th.

The Beatles were no longer seen as a pop band that made teenagers scream. They proved to be serious, talented songwriters and musicians. They were respected by fans of all ages and musicians of all styles.

The Beatles made rock music an art form. In doing so they opened the doors for more artists who continue to experiment with sounds and styles today.

Sgt. Pepper album cover

23

4 Letting IT BE

"At the point we'd finished *Abbey Road*, the game was up. I think we all accepted that."
-George Harrison

In their final few years the Beatles wrote many famous songs about togetherness, peace, and love. Yet the Beatles themselves were growing apart. Each member had different musical interests that moved him in exciting new directions. Eventually they found being in the band more of a job than a joy.

They formed their own record label, Apple, but John, Paul, George, and Ringo were artists, not businessmen. They struggled to manage the new label. Poor money management only increased tensions.

In 1968 George Harrison became the first Beatle to record a solo album. It featured a great deal of Indian-style music. John followed with an album he made with Yoko Ono, an artist whom he later married. The Beatles recorded three more albums before announcing they were done as a band in April 1970.

Abbey Road was released in 1969. It was as fine a farewell album as could be imagined. In one of the last songs, "The End," John, Paul, and George sing in harmony:

Abbey Road album cover

"And in the end, the love you take
is equal to the love you make."

After the Beatles

After the band broke up, each Beatle stayed in music. John often wrote songs about topics such as religion, the Vietnam War (1959–1975), and politics. His most beloved song is "Imagine." It remains an **anthem** for peace around the world. Over steady piano music, John asks the listener to imagine a world with no wars. "You may say I'm a dreamer," he sings. "But I'm not the only one. I hope someday you'll join us, and the world will live as one." John died on December 8, 1980. A mentally ill man waiting outside John's New York City apartment building shot him.

George Harrison's solo work had him raising questions about the spiritual world. "My Sweet Lord" and "What Is Life?" were two such songs. He was one of the first rock stars to create a benefit concert. George produced the 1971 Concert For Bangladesh. The event raised millions of dollars to aid the starving people of this Middle-Eastern country. In 1988 he recorded as part of a **super-group**, the Traveling Wilburys. This group featured two of George's idols, Bob Dylan and Roy Orbison. George died in 2001 from cancer.

Strawberry Fields, the John Lennon Memorial in Central Park, New York City

anthem: a popular song that comes to be a symbol for a particular point of view

The Beatles, 1969

super-group: a special musical project that brings together great musicians from different well-known bands

Ringo Starr had a number of successful pop singles in the 1970s. He also starred in a few comedy films and the *Thomas The Tank* children's TV show. In 1992 he created a **nostalgia** super-group called the All-Starr Band. He formed this band with other rockers from the 1960s and 1970s. Ringo Starr and his All-Starr Band continue to tour.

Paul McCartney recorded 24 solo albums, plus seven albums for orchestra and five **electronica** albums. In January 2014 he and Ringo performed together at the **Grammy Awards**. At that ceremony, the Beatles were given the Lifetime Achievement Award. Paul and Ringo smiled as they received the honor for making music that is still loved throughout the world. It had been 50 years since they'd stepped off a plane with two of their best friends and changed musical history.

Paul McCartney and Ringo Starr perform together at the Grammys on January 27, 2014.

Chart Topper

The best-selling Beatles single of all time is "Hey Jude," released in August of 1968. It starts as a gentle and encouraging song for anyone going through a bad time. "Take a sad song and make it better," Paul sings in the first verse. The seven-minute song builds and builds, adding choir-like harmony and eventually an entire orchestra. It remains a rock 'n' roll classic with a message that, like so much of the Beatles' music, never grows old.

nostalgia: describes a longing for the past

electronica: dance music featuring the use of machines called synthesizers, electronic drums, and samples of other recorded music

Grammy Awards: an annual music awards celebration that honors the year's best music, as voted on by other professionals in the music business

Glossary

anthem (AN-thuhm)—a popular song that comes to be a symbol for a particular point of view

electronica (ee-lek-TRAH-nih-kuh)—dance music that features the use of machines called synthesizers, electronic drums, and samples of other recorded music

generation (jen-uh-RAY-shuhn)—all the members of a group of people or creatures born around the same time

Grammy Awards (GRAH-mee uh-WARDZ)—an annual music awards celebration that honors the year's best music, as voted on by other professionals in the music business

harmony (HAR-muh-nee)—a set of musical notes played or sung at the same time; the notes blend together to form harmony

harpsichord (HARP-suh-kord)—a keyboard instrument that has wire strings that are plucked

nostalgia (noss-TAL-juh)—describes a longing for the past

psychedelic (sye-kuh-DEL-ick)—a style known for colorful, swirling images and sounds that have a dream-like quality

super-group (SOO-pur-GROOP)—a special musical project that brings together great musicians from different well-known bands

Read More

Dakers, Diane. *The Beatles: Leading the British Invasion.* New York: Crabtree Publishing Company, 2013.

Krull, Kathleen, and Paul Brewer. *The Beatles Were Fab (and They Were Funny).* Boston: Harcourt Children's Books, 2013.

Manning, Mick, and Brita Granström. *The Beatles.* London: Frances Lincoln Children's Books, 2014.

Internet Sites

FactHound offers a safe, fun way to find Internet sites related to this book. All of the sites on FactHound have been researched by our staff.

Here's all you do:

Visit *www.facthound.com*

Type in this code: 9781491418161

 Check out projects, games and lots more at **www.capstonekids.com**

Index